Deep Shade
Flickering Sunlight

Deep Shade
Flickering Sunlight

Selected Haiku of
O Mabson Southard

edited by

Barbara Southard
Randy M. Brooks

Brock Peoples, Student Editor

Brooks Books
Decatur, Illinois

Publication Credits

Grateful acknowledgment is made to the editors of the following publications in which some of these poems appeared in present or earlier versions: *American Haiku; Haiku West; Marsh Grasses and Other Poems* (American Haiku Press, 1967); *Modern Haiku.*

Publishers' Note

Brooks Books is pleased to publish *Deep Shade, Flickering Sunlight: Selected Haiku of O Mabson Southard.*

This collection includes the very best work by one of the leading pioneers exploring the art of haiku in English in the 1960's and 1970's. Southard spent a significant portion of his life's literary work developing his approach to the genre. It is our hope that readers will enjoy these top-quality haiku and develop an appreciation for Southard's significant contributions to the art of haiku in English.

Special thanks are due to several readers who have assisted with the selection of the haiku to be included. Lee Gurga, the editor of *Modern Haiku* magazine, was not only instrumental in encouraging the publication of a collection of O Mabson Southard's haiku, but also supplied a critical reading of the poet's unpublished work. Of course, O's daughter, Barbara Southard, one of Southard's lifelong readers provided the texts, the contexts, careful editing and the love essential to the development of this collection.

Over the last three years, several Millikin University students have been drawn to Southard's haiku and have written critical responses to his work for the Global Haiku Traditions course. Their reader response essays have led to the publication of this collection. Included in the appendix are two examples of reader response essays by Millikin students, Rebecca Langmeyer and Brock Peoples. Special thanks to Brock Peoples who served as student editor for this book during a publishing internship with Brooks Books for the spring of 2002.

O Mabson Southard has continued to receive critical acclaim and the recognition he deserves in anthologies of haiku, but most of his work is out of print or in magazines which are difficult to find. With this collection, his work can now be more fully considered by haiku scholars and enjoyed by contemporary haiku readers.

Randy & Shirley Brooks
Decatur, Illinois
November 20, 2003

First edition available only in
library clothbound binding.

ISBN: 1-929820-05-4

Brooks Books
3720 N. Woodridge Drive
Decatur, Illinois 62526

http://www.familynet.net/~brooksbooks
email: brooksbooks@q-com.com

TABLE OF CONTENTS

APPENDIX

dedicated to

O

The Life and Work of
Ordway Southard

The poet was a man known by many names. He was born Ordway Southard, but during his stay in the Hawaiian Islands in the sixties, he and his wife, Mary, made the fateful decision to enroll in a Hawaiian language class. The professor suggested that they all adopt Hawaiian names, and their friends responded enthusiastically to the new names, O for Ordway and Malia for Mary. Somewhat later, under the influence of feminist thought, O Southard became disenchanted with the use of the patronymic, Southard. He then became Mabelsson Norway (Mabel was his mother's name and Norway was her pet name for him in childhood). His last published works appeared under the name O Mabson Southard.

Ordway was born in Cambridge, Massachusetts on November 29, 1911. He came from an old New England family that traced their ancestry on both sides back to English migrants of the early seventeenth century. His mother's father, Horace Austin, was governor of Minnesota in the late nineteenth century, and Mabel Austin was educated at Oberlin and later took her M.D. at Johns Hopkins at a time when there were few women doctors. She married Elmer Ernest Southard, a professor of psychiatry at Harvard, and the couple had two boys and a girl.

When Ordway was eight years old, his father died of pneumonia while on a trip giving lectures about his work in psychiatry. His mother, a competent woman of forceful personality, dedicated herself to public health work and her three children. As some of the poems in this collection reveal, she was a source of loving support, but Ordway also recalled that she had very high standards for achievement. His elder brother, Austin, developed schizophrenia and killed himself in his late teens. At the time, Ordway felt that undue family pressures for academic success had something to do with his brother's death, but he recognized later in life that schizophrenia has a biochemical component that cannot be blamed on family environment.

After his brother's death, the future poet studied for a year or two at Harvard, where he played on the chess team, but his studies were interrupted when he developed tuberculosis and spent a year in a sanatorium. By the time he recovered, Ordway had decided to resist family pressures for a brilliant career and to cultivate an independent, unconventional lifestyle.

Ordway was very close to his sister, Anne (Nan was his pet name for her), his closest companion and confederate in the games and small conspiracies of childhood. He remembered her as a girl of many talents, who outdid him in such skills as skipping stones over water. It was Anne who introduced her brother to Mary Carr Boggs, a graduate student at Radcliffe, whom he married. The poet later recalled that Anne had been eager for the two of them to become friends, but felt abandoned after they paired off.

Ordway found a lifelong companion in Mary who shared his desire to escape from a life of conformity. She had endured a strict Presbyterian upbringing in a narrow minded and racist environment in South Carolina; her intellectual brilliance had enabled her to obtain scholarships and escape the confines of her family. They were married in 1936, and had one child, a girl, in 1945.

After their marriage, Ordway and Mary traveled to Mexico, where they lived for about a year in the late thirties. In the forties, they moved to Alabama and participated in the civil rights movement in the South. They were both attracted to Marxist political thought in this period. Ordway attended the University of Alaska in the late forties. In 1949, the couple moved to New York City.

The poet did not have a career in the conventional sense. Indeed, he believed that striving for money and success stunted real intellectual growth and made emotional growth impossible. Although he earned a degree in anthropology at the University of Alaska, and developed an abiding interest in other cultures, the poet never pursued a career in his academic specialty. Whenever his family needed money he took up a job but not with a vocation in mind. While in New York City in the fifties he developed a moving van business and also published a fascinating magazine about chess called *Leaves of Chess*.

He was equally unconventional in his attitude to marriage. Although Ordway and Mary (later known to both friends and family as O and Malia) were devoted to each other, theirs was an open relationship that did not preclude other passionate attachments. The couple shared a deep love for nature, literature, the arts and social justice. Friends who accompanied them on frequent jaunts into the wilderness remember their endurance and enthusiasm as they embarked on adventurous treks to high peaks, deep ravines, treacherous river crossings, and precipitous waterfalls. In later years, the poet preferred literary pursuits, but he was supportive of his wife's work for ecological causes and the rights of indigenous peoples in Hawaii and British Columbia.

After Southard became disenchanted with the ideological rigidities of leftist political thought in the fifties, he was drawn to Oriental philosophy and literature. He was deeply interested in Taoism and Zen as well as Japanese and Chinese art and poetry. Oriental philosophy was in tune with his deepest instincts, because it offered an alternative to the Western emphasis on the conquest of nature. He studied Japanese, but probably read most of the Japanese haiku masters in English translation. His first haiku verses were published in *American Haiku* in 1963.

In 1961, Southard and his family moved to Hawaii. The move reflected his desire to become closer acquainted with Oriental culture and thought. His daughter attended the University of Hawaii and his wife, who had earned a masters degree in education at Barnard in New York, pursued a career in teaching. The decade spent in Hawaii (1961 to 1971) was crucial to his development as a poet. He acquired an abiding love for the flora and fauna of the islands, its culture and people. His first and only book of poetry, *Marsh Grasses*, was published in 1967. His verses also appeared in the haiku journals *American Haiku, Haiku West* and *Modern Haiku*.

Beginning in the late sixties, the poet was also influenced by feminist thought, although he rejected any attempt to downplay the differences between men and women. He believed that masculine striving for material success and power had run amuck, creating a nightmarish world with little room for intuitive feminine kinship with nature. For Southard, it was not so much a matter of equality of the sexes as restoring the power of the feminine (or the *yin* of Taoist thought).

In 1971, after visiting friends on Vancouver Island in British Columbia, the poet decided to move there. He was charmed by the natural beauty of Vancouver Island and impressed with the cultural life of Victoria and the civic sense of its residents. Perhaps he was reminded of certain aspects of the New England of his childhood. He lived in Victoria until he died on May 6, 2000.

In an autobiographical sketch that accompanied the publication of some of his verses in 1974 in *The Haiku Anthology,* the poet declared: "The joys and terrors of my shade-loving life are nature, womanhood, and words." Southard strongly believed that haiku should be based on concrete experience, and his keen observation of nature was cultivated in the course of frequent wanderings in the wilderness. He rejected literary criticism that emphasized the symbolic in his poetry. Whatever symbolism might be construed by others, the poet avowed that the verses he wrote flowed from concrete moments of enhanced sensibility.

Southard was convinced that the capacity of our senses to perceive the natural world must be cultivated by living simply. The individual caught in the pursuit of ambition and material possessions has neither the time nor the inclination to do so. According to the poet, it is independence of mind and heart that allows feelings to flow deep and true. The words follow.

—Barbara Southard
April, 2002

MORNING MIST

A marshy meadow;
in the salt air, this morning,
the smell of new hay

In the onshore breeze
marsh grasses wave with the masts
of a hidden boat

Here behind a dune
the wind begins to lay bare
a human jaw bone

Here in soft beach sand
    the old cow's cloven hoofprint—
        full of sea water

One breaker crashes . . .
    As the next draws up, a lull—
        and sandpiper cries

The waves now fall short
　　of a stranded jellyfish . . .
　　　In it shines the sky

In the dark water
　　bright grains of phosphorescence—
　　　and a few deep stars

Steadily it snows . . .
Under the shadowy pines—
where are the shadows?

Snow no longer falls;
left in the sky, this morning—
a scatter of stars

On the top fence rail
    he lights, knocking off some snow—
        a common sparrow

A bar of iron—
    upon the old wall, it throws
        so soft a shadow!

Now the leaves are still—
    and only the mockingbird
        lets the moonlight through!

To the cloud-barred moon
the wind, stirring a dark vine,
lays bare a melon

Through pines, a short sigh;
up from tangled sugarcanes
a listless rustle

The path leads nowhere;
whoever made it and why—
no one seems to know

This misty morning—
  adrift on the high water
    an empty canoe

Holding out her hands
  the two-year-old starts to trail
    a courting pigeon

Past the rising moon
owls hoot to one another—
and an apple falls

In darkness the cliffs
echo moonlit waterfalls . . .
A mockingbird sings

Across the still lake
   through upcurls of morning mist—
     the cry of a loon!

Motionless the reeds
and the reflected heron . . .
Somewhere a fish jumps

A patter of rain . . .
The lily pad undulates
on widening rings

Out from under shore
　　drifts a single summer cloud
　　　deep in lake water

Trailing the canoe
　　out into the windswept lake—
　　　a pair of muskrats

Nodding, a rush gleams . . .
   Up from dark open water
   one edge of the moon

Rubbing the canoe
   moonlit reeds conceal a nest
   of soft goose-gabble

From wind and moonlight
   the bridge shelters the river—
   and this leaky boat

Thick with stars, the sky;
　　from the laden pines, a sigh—
　　　and showers of snow

Under the new moon
　　thin-edged with evening sunlight
　　　a snowy hilltop

Beyond mountain pines
　　and ledges of bare granite—
　　　a misty valley

Through the young aspens
  darkness brings a cool east wind
  and flickering stars

In the mountain breeze
  the long slender branch still sways
  with the porcupine

Against the cloud-drift
the wooded cliffs lean forward—
and release a hawk!

Through deep pine-soughing
and my sudden drowsiness—
the sound of a brook

Under dense hemlocks
reflected in the dark pool
an Indian-pipe

Up from quiet ferns
        querying the dusky air
            a shy mosquito

The clear morning moon—
        into its blotches has crept
            the blue of the sky!

Rocky, this hilltop;
   rising behind leafless trees
      a single white cloud

To the dry corn-shock
   the cloud shadow brings a chill—
      and a faint rustle

Still sunlit, one tree;
  into the mountain shadow
    it lets fall a leaf

In a muddy rut
   dark water harbors visions
   of the Milky Way

Grove to grove, tonight,
   the Milky Way's dark potholes—
   and the hoots of owls

Slipping through the pines
on its way to meet the moon—
a weft of thin mist

Moonlight: up they loom
from the dark water—the posts
of the rotting pier

Company tonight!
Chirping from the window sill
a pair of crickets

DISTANT MOUNTAINS

Just crumbling stone walls—
and still the catbird recalls
the swing of a gate

As its final gifts
the old tree bears a small leaf
and a large apple

At the window, sleet . . .
Here in the dark old farmhouse—
the squeaking of mice

Dull blue now, the snow;
deep in one window, the glow
of the setting sun

On the old maple
an open sugar-bucket
full of rain water

Hearing a whinny
the old horse leaves the dust bath
to the young sparrow

DEEP SOUTHEAST

Basking there eye-deep
the bayou's alligator
suddenly thrashes

Deep call-notes of frogs—
and from high in the swamp-elm
a tree toad's dry trill

Down, now, the live oak . . .
Among the wakened echoes—
a turkey's gobble

Over the dark wall
    the moon's foreglow brings the scent
    of blooming jasmine

In moonlit silence
    the mockingbird changes trees . . .
    The lovers lie still

Setting, now, the moon . . .
    Up out of a darkened gulch
    in full cry—the dogs

Far Northwest

Caribou-barrens . . .
   Out from the distant mountains
   wanders a shower

Staining the driftwood
   rain-patter dots the river
   with a shoal of rings

An Eskimo grave;
   beneath the leaning timbers
   a kayak paddle

Over the tundra
  pale butterflies come streaming
    through a sun-shower

Cloudless, now, the sky . . .
  Clinging to this blueberry—
    a tinted raindrop

Here among the stones
  the sand beach comes to an end—
    and I lose the trail

ISLAND SOUTH 1

Here strips of driftweed
cast their water-bent shadows
on a basking shark

To the outrigger
the mountain breeze brings a hint
of ginger-blossoms

Under the cool sway
of rustling coconut trees
the women whisper

From the waterfall
over to the shower-tree
a sudden rainbow

On the lagoon, dusk;
nearly full, the misty moon—
and the girl's dim smile

Rising from the sea
past dark-profiled rainy cliffs
a dense cloud of stars

ISLAND SOUTH 2

Parting the bushes
 I find myself on the brink
 of a deep valley

Within the leaf-whirl
 lying on the cave's dirt floor
 a wild pig's dry bones

Here below the falls
 the candlenut leaf sails off
 among the bubbles

Swinging a stout pole
the old man strives to bring down
a green coconut

Up from the sea cave
through holes in its rocky roof
a fresh burst of surf

Down the coral slope
disappearing in the gloom
a pale yellow fish

In the sea, sunset . . .
    On the dark dune, a bright fringe
    of waving grasses

One banana leaf
    gives to its dark untorn mate
    shivers of moonlight

On yesterday's cairn
    under tonight's moonflowers
    I place a dark stone

Stretching its red rays
across old flows of lava—
up comes the huge sun

With sudden loud whacks
the giant bamboos renew
their swaying battle

Again a sharp cry—
and again the tropic-bird
soars past the sea cliff

Out of the smooth sea
dawn brings the slender moon's tip—
and a shark's grey fin

Into a wave, out—
and into the next, and out—
a school of dolphins

Storm-dark, now, the waves . . .
Far astern, sunshine lingers
on a leaning sail

Left by the backwash
on a palm-fringed sandy beach—
the moon's reflection

Purple-brown, the sky;
yellow-black, the frantic sea:
both—now lost in rain

Out from the huge wave
comes a sudden jet of spray—
and a flying fish

With sharp leaf-shadows
    the cove's leaning palms cross-hatch
    the beached coconut

Up the quiet beach
    the broken wave sends a sweep
    of swerving water

Over the tide pool
    another wave's high flung spray—
    and a tattler's cry

Waving his great claw
the crab glides down the sand beach
into the high surf

From the surf, moonrise . . .
Between waves, the girls compare
their foamy bosoms

Trained on my bare feet
swinging round the dark lagoon—
the moon's narrow wake

ISLAND SOUTH 4

The pool-moon's halo
encloses a fitful star—
and a croaking frog!

Flaunting skirts of grass
beneath the high moon, the girls
dance with their shadows

With the candlenuts
clinging to the branch, a dove
and her fledgling brood

Out of the pine-duff
creeps a long prickly-pear plant
with yellow blossoms

Deeper in the cave
the diminishing twilight—
and the smell of earth

Swift, the cloud shadows . . .
Now as the first sweeps over—
it seems to linger

On the firelit smoke
shadows of yet unburnt trees
tremble and stagger

Past the smoke column
lit up by my new-fed fire—
the sweep of an owl

Spanning the rapids
half-hidden by upthrown mist—
a new-fallen tree

Cloud-free, now, the sun . . .
   Sipping at the puddle's edge—
      a new butterfly

Climbing the cane stalks
   the mango tree's deep shadow
      engulfs a tassel

Still the stormwind blows—
   and still the empty sky grows
      bluer and bluer!

From the high meadow
losing itself in the mist
a plover's wild call

With the girl's greeting
through the leaves of the wild vine—
a sudden cool breeze

Against shower-clouds
the hilltop jacarandas
have burst into bloom

Now beneath bright haze
the valley's transparent air
deepens to purple

Steadily eastward
the cloud peak carries its trace
of evening sunlight

From the steep trail's turn
one leaf of the *koa* tree
conceals the new moon

Young coconut trees . . .
    Through their leaves, with tonight's wind,
        a flashing of stars

From rain-wet bamboos
    aslant in the sudden breeze—
        an aftershower

Over dark stone walls
    the swaying coconut leaf
        sprinkles its moonlight

DEEP SHADE, FLICKERING SUNLIGHT

A Drove

Down the moonlit slope
a drove of swift cloud-shadows
brings a running horse

Shrill, the mare's whinny . . .
Rippling above the grasses—
her long mane and tail

As her stallion rears
and she prances out of reach—
the mare stoops to graze

With hooves water-hushed
the stallion's mares ford the stream—
and churn it to foam

Plump with foal, the mares
munch at shadowy grasses
aglint with moondew

Dawn-grey, the meadow . . .
Wading through a stretch of mist—
the colt and his dam

DAWN

In our tryst-oak's den
    for exchange of gifts, I find
        my chuckling sister

With the lily pads
    in our tryst-cove, the breeze lifts
        my sister's leaf skirt

Seeing herself seen
    atop the snowy hemlock—
        the raven flies off

So my eyes may rest—
   my comet-watching sister
      lets me comb her hair

Chanting, the pond's frogs . . .
   Among the lilies' dark pads—
      the twinkle of stars

In the tinge of dawn
   behind the bending grasses—
      the slender moon's tip

DARK HEMLOCKS

Through the lofty arch
between cliff and waterfall
the moon looks misty

Up through dark hemlocks
that overhang the valley—
the river's moonlight

Biding our dark tryst
by the wild shore, my sister
listens to the loons

Dark pad to dark pad—
one pond-lily's frog describes
an arc of moonlight

With bosoms afloat
the girls wade toward each other—
and catch the pool's moon

As the dark frogs chant—
faint ripples begin to lap
at my moonlit boat

LEAFLESS WOODS

Here in our tryst-glade
    my sister's dark eyes reflect
        falling maple leaves

Through the pines, a lull . . .
    For now—the punctual crunch
        of my own snowshoes

In the chilly air
    drifting through the leafless woods—
        a few plum petals

Climbing toward the clouds
through the new leaves, I look down
at banks of old snow

Mingled in the falls—
the water tones of others
higher and lower

Her field-heated form
grove-cooled, my laughing sister
shudders in my arms

FAINT ROLLING THUNDER

For my sister's horse
I listen in the stillness—
and hear my own heart

As yet shadowy
under dawn's misty half moon—
the swampside haymow

Steeped in river mist
the motionless cottonwoods—
and their reflections

Faint rolling thunder . . .
　　Out from the hills come dust whirls
　　　and big drops of rain

In daytime darkness
　　the rain-blurred windows rattle—
　　　and the kettle storms

Thronging the puddles
　　along this deserted road—
　　　a party of clouds

GLEAMING SUNKEN STONES

Trees arch the river—
and the deliberate flight
of a white heron

Gleaming sunken stones . . .
With her shadow, the catfish
turns them off and on

Washed from the shell mound
by the cedar-shaded waves—
the bones of a child

Under the live oak:
  deep shade, flickering sunlight—
  and a wild turkey

On a leaf, a leaf
  casts a swaying green shadow—
  and the tree frog sings!

Chased by butterflies
  my laughing sister's flat stone
  skips more times than mine

Tripping Along the Path

This morning's rainbow
   shares its deep violet edge
      with the misty moon

Again shower-wet
   the lichen-spotted boulder
      reflects the sky's blue

From leafless plum trees
   over the thundering falls—
      a storm of petals

A trim, quiet girl
comes tripping along the path—
and I ask the way

Sparkling in the air
at sunset, fine bouyant rain
half hides the dark cliffs

Down to dark leaf-mold
the falling dogwood petal
carries its moonlight

WILD STRAWBERRIES

Here on the hillside
sunrise is just ripening
some wild strawberries

Still followable
through this morning's cling of dew—
my sister's green trail

The old rooster crows . . .
Out of the mist come the rocks
and the twisted pine

The door bursts open . . .
   Into the hut, the gust brings
      a green maple leaf

Catching us at tryst—
   our mother gathers bindweed
      for my sister's hair

Over the lost cows
   milling about the meadow—
      a flock of egrets

TREE HOUSE

Round the idling drakes
    and the duck that happens by—
    storm cloud reflections

As hailstones pelt her—
    the sitting catbird, eyes closed,
    points her bill straight up

Rocking our tree house
    the rainstorm lulls me to sleep
    in my sister's arms

Dawn, and still raining . . .
For me, my sister recalls
her dreams of water

On the roof, rain-roar . . .
From under the dripping eaves—
phoebe nestlings' cries

Perching, bolt upright—
the crow lets the rain water
trickle from her tail

Rocky Peak

Overwhelmed by mist
the rocky peak struggles out—
and sinks back under

My snow down her neck
my sister laughs, and shudders,
and kisses my mouth

Staining the cliff dark
with afternoon meltwater—
a cornice of snow

Lodged in the plunge-pool
the trunk of a broken tree
parts the waterfall

Under the cool pines
the path dips round a boulder
and climbs to a ledge

By her childhood name
I call and call my sister—
and so do the cliffs

Falling Snow

By the pine-fringed pool
  my mother, clothed in her hair,
    points me out mushrooms

Keeping our grove-tryst
  I find my sister's dropped clothes—
    and hear her laughter

Wringing from the oak
  spiral showers of dry leaves—
    on come whirls of dust

Hunched up, the sparrow . . .
    In the bare bush, the cold wind
        keeps ruffling her breast

Through the pines, a lull . . .
    For now—the punctual crunch
        of my own snowshoes

Over my campfire—
    flakes of soot whirl together
        with the falling snow

WILD VINE

Dusk-free, the peach bloom . . .
Over the valley's wild trees—
daybreak's tinted clouds

On the rain-damped ground
blossom shadows reappear—
steadily bobbing

Again the wind slants
the cypresses' longbeard moss—
and the streaks of rain

Flirting, the dove pair . . .
From the bouyant branch, they fly
their separate ways

With my sister's voice
greeting me through the wild vine—
a sudden cool breeze

The moon clears the pines . . .
Exposed, a water lily
begins to open

Ring of Mushrooms

Mirrored by the spring
under the pines, a cluster
of Indian-pipes

Drowsy with pine-roar
I feel my surf-cool sister
put shells to my ears

Napping, my sister . . .
Each time our tryst-pines murmur—
her lashes quiver

To the moon-blanched grass
　　within the ring of mushrooms—
　　　my sister lures me

By her side, I wake . . .
　　Still above my sister's breast—
　　　the top of the moon

In our dark tryst-spring
　　my sister shows me her self—
　　　and a dawn-tipped spruce

A Green Lichen

Now a green lichen
    deprives the stone catamount
      of one glaring eye

Drawn to the deep moss
    on our mother's mother's grave—
      I join my sister

Deepening, the dusk . . .
    Atop the hemlock's dead stub—
      the shape of an owl

In the garden pool,
    dark and still, a stepping stone
        releases the moon

At our dawn brook-bath
    blush creeps from my sister's brow
        right down to her toes

Against the leaf mold
    I can make out the woodhen—
        but only her eye!

WISP OF MIST

The sound of an axe . . . ?
Tumbling in the rocks, a brook . . .
The mountain stillness

In the wisp of mist
clinging to the leafless tree—
a frozen apple

Now it starts to sleet . . .
Toward mine, my trudging sister
turns her smitten face

Receiving a stone
the trailside thaw-pool shudders—
and reclaims the sky

From deep in the spring
clear reflections rise to meet
falling plum petals

With the wild vine's leaves
our rising tryst-moon dapples
my sister's bare breast

WINDSWEPT GRASSLAND

Flush with the treetops
a wedge of windswept grassland
divides the ravines

With a sudden snort
    the pregnant mare curls her lip
      round a wisp of grass

Up, the laughing girl . . .
    As her braid swings to his back—
      the horse flicks his tail

Fogbound on the dunes
I listen with my sister
for distant breakers

Stiff, now, the sea breeze . . .
Rippling under ragged clouds—
a marshy meadow

From the cliff's ledges
   gloomy groves of wind-shaped pines
   echo the surf's roar

Close to ocean-doom
   the river whispers farewells
   to its drowning banks

with Malia Southard

Tranquil, now, the lake . . .
    Once more a steady mountain
        rests on steady clouds

Forgetting bluets
    he's just brought me—he buys me
        with the summer sky

                with Malia Southard

In the afterglow
    pinking the clear mountaintop—
        snow-clad cinder cones

Round the lake's thawn glade
    flickering in the sunlight—
        a flight of wild ducks

Snow peaks hear the flute . . .
Potato-blossom girls dance
on the high pampa

with Malia Southard

Off with that old cloak . . .
Let her wild skirts ebb and flow
round her dancing feet

with Malia Southard

Aswirl, the brook's flood—
   and the tail of the squirrel
    on her pine-crossing

After a long wait
   the wild goose raises her head
    above the tall grass

From the birch forest
round the crows' pine, mist rises
to their scraggy nest

Imaged, she finds one
grey hair—and tosses pebbles
into the dark pool

with Malia Southard

A stupendous wind
  lays me naked in a field—
    and I laugh aloud

Boating, we make love . . .
Her sudden joy sweeps us both
through a batch of waves

Galloping her mare
  the cowgirl suddenly screams—
  and tingles my spine

Stealing through the cave
  new snow's reflected moonlight
  wakes a dog's deep howl

At Wild Girl's bosom
I listen—and hear the pound
of distant breakers

Wine-dark springs your hair . . .
Waves flounce their own underskirts—
and we glimpse the reef

Shredding purple crests
from its own breakers, dawn's gale
besprinkles the dunes

Curbing her stallion
  she sometimes hands me the reins—
  and kisses my cheek

Apple of mine eye . . .
  I'm in the pupil of hers—
  diminutively

Blooming daffodils . . .
   They're all blooming, except one—
   the bloody laggard!

She likes floating nude
with nakeds . . . But a tadpole's
nuzzle startles her

At their shorecliff tryst
the lad's tongue fishes for hers—
and gets gentle bites

With the palm grove's fronds
the elephant's ears wave . . . She
dozes where she stands

To the single moon
  she opposes her breasts twain—
    and her babe's buttocks

READER RESPONSE ESSAYS
Millikin University

Haiku of American Poet
O Mabson Southard

A Reader's Response Essay
by
Brock Peoples

O Mabson Southard began writing haiku in response to a new found interest in eastern thought; especially Taoism and Zen Buddhism. The Zen principles of "wordless" (brevity and incompleteness), "suchness" (things are included within themselves, just as they are), "nothing special" (ordinary events and things), "season word," "selfless" (the haiku are not about the author), and "oneness" (everything is connected) that are discussed in Eric Amann's *The Wordless Poem: A Study of Zen in Haiku* are prevalent in O Southard's work. The poet's daughter, Barbara Southard, writes that he "strongly believed that haiku should be based on concrete experience, and his keen observation of nature was cultivated in the course of frequent wanderings in the wilderness." This combination of Zen principles and a close relationship with the natural world led O Mabson Southard to write a large number of haiku dealing almost completely with nature and natural beauty.

The following are selections of O Southard's haiku that I especially appreciate from this collection.

> On the top fence rail
> he lights, knocking off some snow—
> a common sparrow

This haiku presents an image of a fresh snowfall. The writer is looking out over the scene and happens to notice a common sparrow landing, knocking snow to the ground as he does. This event is small and mundane. Even the bird is nothing special, just a common sparrow.

Just crumbling stone walls—
and still the catbird recalls
the swing of a gate

In this haiku, the writer has come across crumbled walls, which is all that remains of an old homestead. I myself have come across a similar ghost: the remains of steel rafters and a concrete pump house foundation forming one side of a spring's basin. The feeling that such places radiate is one of longing and of remembrance of days long gone, but also of serenity. Nature reclaims what was once hers. Southard describes a scene in which a catbird gives a call resembling a sound that may once have been made by the long-gone gate.

A bar of iron—
upon the old wall, it throws
so soft a shadow!

This haiku is an excellent demonstration of Zen. The "suchness" of the image of the iron bar and its shadow is its own meaning. Also, the idea of "nothing special" is here, as well as "selfless," in that the author does not put himself in the image. What I appreciate about this haiku is the contradiction between the cold hard iron and its soft shadow. This haiku gives me a feeling of summer when the window shades are drawn up and the windows are open to let the breeze in. The iron bar's soft shadow also conveys a sense of warmth for me, another contradiction to the cold steel.

In the sea, sunset . . .
On the dark dune, a bright fringe
of waving grasses

The dune's grasses are illuminated from the setting Hawaiian sun in this haiku. The sunset is painting the sea, but shadow already lies over the land. However, the grasses fringing the sand dune are still basking in the sun's warmth and light. This haiku demonstrates Southard's ability to observe details and write haiku on events that the average person does not notice.

Past the smoke column
lit up by my new-fed fire—
the sweep of an owl

I imagine Southard on one of his many excursions into the wilds with his wife and their friends, sitting by a small but blazing fire with a small note pad on his knee. He leans back and closes his eyes for a moment and inhales the clean air of the wilderness. As he opens his eyes, he glimpses an owl passing swiftly from the darkness and back again by the light of the fire. At this moment, he writes this haiku, giving us one of the few haiku he wrote on nature that are not "selfless."

Boating, we make love . . .
Her sudden joy sweeps us both
through a batch of waves

This poem captures the passion and joy of union that can come from physical love when the lover loses himself in the pleasure of his loved one. The woman's orgasm is strong enough to carry both of them through a batch of waves. This haiku treats the act of making love as something beautiful that the couple is sharing with each other, and with the sea around them.

The old rooster crows . . .
Out of the mist come the rocks
and the twisted pine

This haiku is probably my favorite out of all of Southard's work. It combines serenity and revelation through a morning mist. The crowing of the rooster places the reader automatically at dawn, with the mist reinforcing the image. The rocks and the pine are revealed slowly as the mist moves through the valley. Everything is alive with the movement of the mist.

So my eyes may rest—
my comet-watching sister
lets me comb her hair

According to Barbara Southard, O and his sister were extremely close throughout their lives. This haiku captures that closeness as the two share an intimate moment while comet-watching. Southard's eyes have grown tired of straining to see the comet, so, he combs his sister's hair instead. She allows him to do so as she continues to watch the comet in the sky above. This haiku is a wonderful moment illustrating the beautiful relationship Southard shared with his sister.

Chanting, the pond's frogs . . .
Among the lilies' dark pads—
the twinkle of stars

Frogs have always been a favorite topic for haiku writers and Southard is not without his frog haiku. These small creatures that are so often ignored in our busy day-to-day lives often fill the night with enchanting music. In this haiku, Southard is painting the image of the frogs' song at night, with the stars splashed across the heavens and reflecting from the pond.

The haiku of O Southard are excellent in their structure, language, wordings, and significance of moments. Southard is a master at capturing haiku moments that show us the little things that we often miss as well as the endless beauty of nature. He succeeded in writing excellent haiku in 5-7-5 form that have stood the test of time. It has been 35 years since the publication of O Southard's one and only collection of poetry, *Marsh Grasses*, but his work speaks clearly to haiku writers and readers of today.

—Brock Peoples
Millikin University
April 2002

O Mabson Southard's Haiku

A Reader's Response Essay
by
Rebecca Langmeyer

Sitting down to read poetry, one can only imagine the life full of experiences that lies behind the expression that is being read. Perhaps the writer was a great scientist, a stay-at-home mother, or a philosopher. Reading a particular work, the mind of the reader is able to take words that meant so much to the writer, and manipulate them to create a meaning unique to their own life situation.

The writer whose works I have chosen to study is O Mabson Southard. Although it is unfortunate that I was unable to talk with Mr. Southard about his haiku, it allows for the true meaning of his work to remain a mystery. His readers may continue to create a life through his work and imagine from where he found his words.

As I considered Mr. Southard's life, I imagined the beauty that he found in the simplicity of nature that, perhaps, came from life through the Great Depression. Looking at a time in history where the smallest of things were appreciated, it can be imagined that Mr. Southard was able to see the beauty in simplicity. Perhaps, this underlying theme may be seen in his work. Whether creating a disturbing or breath-taking moment, each haiku captures the occurrences in nature that, so often, we take for granted in the routine of our busy days.

Although Mr. Southard's haiku may be read in many ways and may create a series of memories, I will share with you what I get from the following works.

Snow no longer falls;
    left in the sky, this morning—
        a scatter of stars

This haiku made me think of Christmas Eve, leaving church after a late night candlelight service. There is so much hope and wonder in the air. As I read this, I thought of leaving church to find the deep blanket of new fallen snow and the bright stars lighting up the Christmas sky. The picture that I imagine is breath-taking. The moment, as I see it captured, is one of wonder and simple beauty.

The path leads nowhere;
    whoever made it and why—
        no one seems to know

When I read this haiku, my mind went to a hike in the woods. One of my favorite things to do is hike at a local forest preserve in my hometown. Walking through the woods, there is always something new to be seen. One time, I found a path that was not well-defined. For a change of pace, I chose to follow it. Eventually, the path ended and at its ending point was nothing specific. It made me wonder for what the path was made and who had created it. This haiku made me think of this moment and the feeling that I had once I found that the end of the path was nothing more than was to be found along the other paths. This haiku gives me a sense of loneliness and sadness. It creates a mood that is both serene and melancholic as the reader thinks about the unmarked path.

Across the still lake
    through upcurls of morning mist—
        the cry of a loon!

This haiku is very peaceful and calming. It makes me think of early morning, right after daybreak. Perhaps the location is in the mountains and steam is rising from the mountain lake. Reading this, I can sense the serenity of being in the moment. All is quiet and asleep in the world, and then it is suddenly brought to life with the cry of the loon. It calls as if waking up the world for the new day. I liked this haiku for the calm mood that it creates and the way in which it pulls a reader into that moment.

In the garden pool,
dark and still, a stepping stone
releases the moon

Reading this, I thought about a quiet summer evening, taking a walk in a garden. Walking along, as you look into the pool, you glance at a stepping stone and at the moon's reflection in it. This moment is both calm and romantic, depending upon the company of the writer. Looking into the water, the writer clearly sees the beauty of the night, and it is almost assumed that he is with a lover. That context allows for the enhancement of the moment that is created. I liked this haiku because of the atmosphere that it creates and the variety of ways that it might be interpreted.

Thick with stars, the sky;
from the laden pines, a sigh—
and showers of snow

This haiku made me think of walking along on a warmer winter's night. Again, I assume that the writer is with a lover as they walk. Looking up, they note the stars and perhaps search for constellations. As they search, the wind blows slightly and, with it, the trees send down a shower of snow over the lovers. This haiku allows for the imagination to take over as it fills in the blank spots in the moment.

Mirrored by the spring
under the pines, a cluster
of Indian-pipes

This haiku, I felt, gave a sense of tradition. It contrasted the newness of the spring and the tradition of the Indian pipes. Perhaps the pipes had been there for years, yet nature continued to go on. I felt as though Mr. Southard did a wonderful job at creating a representation of the cycle of life through this haiku.

At the window, sleet . . .
    Here in the dark old farmhouse—
        the squeaking of mice

This haiku was the one I found to be the least about nature. As Southard's readers can see, however, it too includes nature with the mouse moving about. This haiku creates a calm, warm feeling. The subject is sitting out of the rain, perhaps sitting at a window watching it. I imagine, when reading it, that all is quiet, aside from the pitter-patter of the rain. Suddenly, a mouse squeaks, breaking the silence. I would suppose that such a situation would evoke a variety of responses, based on fears of mice. I, however, see it as calming and rather funny that such a little creature can sound so huge when put in the quietest of places.

    On the top fence rail
        he lights, knocking off some snow—
            a common sparrow

This haiku is very simple, yet it creates a very vivid picture. It notes the perching of a bird during the winter. I see this haiku as being set in the Midwest, though that may be from my experience and not the actual context from which this haiku was taken. I particularly enjoyed this haiku as it gives a sense of hope for the spring ahead, yet captures the simplicity of the moment.

Mr. Southard's haiku are treasured by readers all over the world. The simple beauty, present in Mr. Southard's haiku will not be soon forgotten.

—*Rebecca Langmeyer*
Millikin University
Spring 2000